# Tax Saving Strategies

# Tax Saving Strategies

## Patrick Weinert

ISBN-13: 9781091494060
ISBN-10: 1091494060

# Disclaimer

The views presented in this book are those of the author and do not necessarily represent the views of the United States Marine Corps, the Department of Defense (DOD), or its components. No portion of this book may be reproduced without the written permission of the author. The author is not a licensed financial advisor, and he does not engage in the business of licensed financial planning. The reader should consult with a financial advisor before completing any recommendations from this book. The author shares his own ideas and opinions about personal finance in general. This book does not offer individualized or personalized advice attuned to any specific portfolio or to any reader's or user's particular needs. The author makes no assurances or predictions of success or failure as a result of the reader's or user's decision to make use of the ideas and opinions offered in this book. As with all financial decisions, past performance is no guarantee of future results. All trademarks, copyrights and other intellectual property that may be included in this book are the properties of their respective owners.

The characterizations that you find in these publications regarding various third parties—for example, tax preparation software—are the opinion of the author and are based on facts that were believed to be accurate at the time of the initial publication of this book. None of the individuals, companies or other entities mentioned in this book have sponsored or endorsed the author in any way, and there is no affiliation of any kind between them. The author does not guarantee the performance or effectiveness of publicized websites.

Neither the author nor publisher assume any responsibility or liability whatsoever on behalf of any purchaser, reader, or user of this book. No express or implied guarantees or predictions of any kind whatsoever, including the income that may or may not result from use of this book, are made by the author and/or publisher.

# Acknowledgments

I owe so much to my family and friends. My father, Philip Weinert, quoted in this book, is my personal hero who taught me the value of individual liberty and hard work. He is always challenging me to be a better person. My mother Sharon Weinert gave me the best childhood a boy could possibly have. My siblings, Christine, Caroline, and Peter are the closest friends I'll ever have. If not for each of them, I would not be where I am today. My brothers-in-law, Eric and Michael, are my role-models for integrity and hard work as outstanding husbands and fathers. My sister-in-law, Stephanie, is an inspiration in her creative skills as a mother and small business owner. My step-mother, Elaine, has been one of my greatest supporters through all my work. Dayna Wolter is one of my very best friends, who continues to support me every day in my quest to help people with their personal finances. I owe her so much for all her moral support, proof-reading, editing, and feedback on my writing. Matt Coast is an invaluable friend and mentor in this work, always providing priceless advice, encouragement, and moral support. Stu Schneiderman has been my business mentor these past two years and I greatly appreciate his guidance and advice. T. Payne created the outstanding artistic cover and design. I offer thanks to many others, including you the reader, who support my writing and publication of this book. I thank God for the daily blessings He provides, including so many supportive people in my family, friends, and professional relationships.

# Contents

# Foreword

I had my first stirrings of interest in personal liberty during childhood, though I couldn't articulate it at the time. Ever since my early years, I knew I would devote my life to helping others achieve liberty. I always thought of liberty as the ability to choose and achieve what fulfills you. Liberty isn't acting on whatever your appetites may desire in the passing moment. For me, liberty has always been the ability to choose what is good for you, not choose whatever you want. Such a topic is deep for me, and definitely beyond the scope of this book. But, since we are social creatures, the question of liberty always relates to the topic of political economy.

Among the many challenges that face societies, taxes are high on the list. They have been with us since the beginning of recorded history. In the modern era, they bring unique challenges, and they are a difficult topic. They aren't just difficult to complete sometimes, as in "I still haven't finished my taxes!" They're difficult to understand, or even justify. Oliver Wendell Holmes, Jr. wrote "Taxes are what we pay for a civilized society." When he wrote this statement, the average tax rate in the United States was 3.5%. Such a statement makes the listener feel a little bit better about paying taxes, but it still leaves a curious dry feeling in one's stomach. Are these taxes needed for the functioning of a just society? How much should we pay in taxes? Are all taxes just? These are good and important questions, but they are difficult and they need to be discussed.

"Pay your fair share of taxes." This is a moral imperative that is proposed by some conscientious tax-payers. Some of it comes from a sense of moral responsibility, some from a sense of fear. Taxes are a reality, but *how much* is the question that continues to present itself. This is a timeless question.

The first truth we must grasp about the topic of taxes is the following:

Taxes are *political*. We may tell ourselves that taxes are what we pay for a civilized society. We may tell ourselves that taxes are for the sake of the common good. We may tell ourselves that our tax money is used to care for the widow and the orphan. But, the truth is that most taxes are not spent on anything related to enhancing a true common good of society. Most taxes are spent on what is beneficial for an elected representative body. This is a hard truth to hear, but it is reality. This does not mean that all taxes are spent on selfish interests. But, much of it is. How much of it is selfish depends on your political viewpoint and your opinion of what forms a just order.

My foreword is not designed to make a political argument. On the contrary, it's to make a moral one. A citizen is only responsible to pay in taxes what the law requires, and nothing more. Paying more or less in taxes does not reflect on one's personal moral standing. In fact, the less a tax-payer pays, *ceteris paribus*, the more that person has in resources to take care of others. The more citizens can reduce their tax bills, the more money they have to support their families. The more an organization can reduce its tax bill, the more it can devote resources to the causes it serves. The more wealth one has, the more self-sufficient that person becomes. The more capable he or she is at helping fellow citizens and society in general.

How a tax-payer arrives at the final tax bill is a matter of skill. Tax law is complicated. But, a tax-payer can use complication to his advantage, if he understands the battlefield. My goal with this book is to help you reduce your taxes to the lowest amount possible. This will give you more resources to support people and causes you care about most. By saving your resources, you are able to make a positive impact on your own liberty, as well as the liberty of others. You'll be able to help those loved ones or disadvantaged people that you serve.

I applaud you in your hard work and desire to save on taxes. I look forward to seeing you continue moving toward those goals you have set for you, your family, and loved ones.

Patrick Weinert
Washington, D.C.
March 21, 2019

# Introduction

*A penny saved is a penny earned.*
– Benjamin Franklin

*A dollar saved is a dollar thirty cents earned. Don't forget about taxes.*
– Philip Weinert

In 2005, I deployed overseas as a United States Marine Corps helicopter pilot for a seven month tour in Iraq. On one overcast day in mid-December, one of my Marines and I went to the chow hall on base to eat breakfast. It was a real treat for both of us, because our schedules did not normally allow us to eat food in the base dining facility. With a few minutes to spare before breakfast, my Marine went to retrieve his clean laundry from the laundry tent. In the interests of time, we went from the laundry tent to the chow hall, so we could get some food and then immediately go back to work. But, once we approached the chow hall, we encountered a problem. The guard at the entrance raised his hand at us and said: "No bags allowed in the chow hall."

This was a real problem. We couldn't leave the laundry outside. We didn't have enough time to take the laundry back to my Marine's tent. We also couldn't give it to someone else, and we weren't allowed to split up.

The restriction on bags was for our safety, and we knew this. If bags were allowed in the facility, an enemy terrorist could bring in a bag of explosives. This could hurt many people.

After a few tense moments of indecision, we came up with an idea. Our uniforms had large cargo pockets on the trousers. I had my Marine take all his laundry out of his laundry bag, and put it into his cargo pockets. I then had him put the bag in his pocket. At that point, now "bag-less," we were allowed to enter the dining facility.

That experience, while seemingly insignificant, left a lasting impression on me. Rules and laws are made for the safety and well-being of a community. However, rules always have unintended consequences. The Law of Unintended Consequences states that actions of people—and especially of government—always have effects that are unintended. This isn't a bad thing, it's just a fact of human nature.

A law to decrease the speed limit on highways may actually make those highways more dangerous when some cars slow down to comply with the law but others continue "speeding" (Galles, 1993). A minimum wage, intended to give workers a minimum amount of pay for their work, may actually prevent those very workers from getting jobs when employers move their businesses to a lower wage market. And if a law says that tenants should be protected against landlords, those landlords may make their occupancy standards so high that tenants with less than perfect credit are unable to live in a desirable area.

The Law of Unintended Consequences applies the most in the realm of taxes. Ask any group of law-abiding citizens if everyone should pay their taxes. The majority will say yes. But ask those same people if they would like a lower tax bill, and the majority will also say yes.

We like to believe that tax law is created with the common good of the community as first priority. But, the truth is that tax law is a snarled mess of regulations compiled over many decades. Historically, tax law's true first priority has been to further political careers. Taxes are *political*. Recognizing this truth will help you frame them in a positive way. The political nature of taxes results in many unintended consequences that come with tax law. And, you can take advantage of some of these consequences. Paying your "fair share" of taxes is required by law, but how you live your life isn't a legal mandate. As a result, creative minds can follow the law in a way that reduces their tax costs. Helping you adopt an effective tax strategy is one of the goals of this book.

Tax strategy is a rarely used term. When most people file their taxes each year, they are in reaction mode. Most people gather their W-2s, 1099s, and other tax forms, and they frantically enter information into a software interface or give it to a Certified Public Accountant (CPA).

You may not be a business owner, or even earn a large income. But, as a working professional, being knowledgeable on your taxes is important. Even if you use tax preparation software or have someone else do your taxes for you, you should be familiar with the tax breaks available to you. If your CPA or tax software make a mistake, you are the one who is responsible.

During my career in the United States Marine Corps, my superiors asked me to manage the Marine Corps budget. This was a challenging job. At the time, the military budget was being cut. I had to shepherd a process where there were different demands for money coming from different parts of the service. In addition to this, higher authority taxed the Marine Corps. In one case, the Department of the Navy levied a tax. In another case, the Office of the Secretary of Defense demanded a tax from all the services. Sometimes these taxes would come with little or no notice. As the lead for the budgeting process, I became skilled at finding ways to reduce taxes or delay their payment.

While I was responsible for managing the budget, our team achieved success with balancing the needs of the service and paying our taxes. After my retirement from the service, I desired to apply my skills to help individuals manage their personal and small business taxes. Organizations and individuals face many similar challenges, especially when it comes to taxes.

The purpose of this book is to help you understand taxes and make them simple for you. Taxes are a reality we all have to live with. Wherever you live, you will always have to pay some taxes. Having a good understanding of your tax is a great way to save money and improve in your own personal finances. In some ways, tax efficiency is the best way to improve your cash flow. You've already earned the money. Now you just have to keep as much as possible.

Frequently, there is a negative connotation associated with minimizing your tax bill. This is criticized as someone not paying "their fair share" of taxes. The truth is that minimizing your tax bill is good, since it allows you to improve your personal financial situation. It also allows you to contribute to the causes you believe in. Improving your personal financial situation is good for you. When you are financially stronger, you can better support your family or those dependent on you. You should never feel guilty for understanding the tax law. You should also never feel guilty for using this knowledge to reduce your tax bill. You are only obligated to pay what the law requires.

This book offers two fundamental goals to strategize on your federal income taxes:

1. Pay the lowest amount of tax possible
2. Pay your tax bill on the due date, and not earlier than necessary

This book will synthesize these goals in a manageable way for you to learn and take action. This is not another book explaining your tax deductions and credits. This book is a unique compilation of several tax strategies you can use to reduce your tax bill. These strategies are not included in tax reference books or tax preparation software. Using these strategies, our aim is to get your tax bill as low as possible, and pay the tax when it's due, and not a day earlier.

# Tax Brackets and Withholding

*The difference between death and taxes is death*
*doesn't get worse every time Congress meets.*
*– Will Rogers*

My friend Stefan from Sweden marvels at what he considers great tax rates when he visits the United States. "If I lived here, I'd be in the 22% tax bracket" he would say. "So I only have to pay 22% of my income in taxes. That's a good deal!"

In Sweden, where Stefan pays 60% of his income in taxes, 22% seemed like a good deal to him. But, this misunderstands what the tax brackets require you to pay.

Our federal taxes are graduated taxes. That means, as you earn more money, you pay a progressively higher tax rate. So, if I am a single tax-payer earning $30,000 per year, I would be in the 12% tax bracket. But, I don't pay 12% of all my pay in taxes. Instead, I'll pay 10% on my first $9,525, and 12% on the next $20,475. So, my total tax bill will be $953 + $2,457 = $3,410. Divide this by $30,000 to see the effective tax rate of 11.37%.

The higher your income rises, the more you are taxed at an increasing rate. If I make $100,000 per year, I'll be taxed at the 24% rate on all income between $82,500 and $100,000. If I earn $400,000 as a married person filing jointly, I'd pay 32% of the income between $315,000 and $400,000 in taxes. Progressive tax rates require some thought to understand what you actually owe. But, you don't have to do the math to figure it out. This is computed for you on tax preparation software. You can also find this by referring to the tax tables in the Internal Revenue Service (IRS) publication (pub) 17. You can find pub 17 on the IRS website at www.irs.gov.

The 2018 tax brackets are listed in Table 1 below.

## Table 1: 2018 Tax Brackets

| Bracket | Single | Married Filing Jointly/Widow(er) | Married Filing Separately | Head of Household |
|---|---|---|---|---|
| 10% | 9,525 | 19,050 | 9,525 | 13,600 |
| 12% | 9,526 – 38,700 | 19,051 – 77,400 | 9,526 – 38,700 | 13,601 – 51,800 |
| 22% | 38,701 – 82,500 | 77,400 – 165,000 | 38,701 – 82,500 | 51,800 – 82,500 |
| 24% | 82,501 – 157,500 | 165,000 – 315,000 | 82,501 – 157,500 | 82,501 – 157,500 |
| 32% | 157,501 – 200,000 | 315,000 – 400,000 | 157,501 – 200,000 | 157,501 – 200,000 |
| 35% | 200,001 – 500,000 | 400,001 – 600,000 | 200,001 – 300,000 | 200,001 – 500,000 |
| 37% | Over 500,000 | Over 600,000 | Over 300,000 | Over 500,000 |

*Filing* your taxes is the act of sending the appropriate forms to the IRS each year to define your total tax bill. You can do this on paper and mail it through the postal mail system; you can use tax preparation software to prepare and file your taxes electronically; or, you can hire a CPA to complete and deliver your taxes to the IRS for you.

How you file your taxes is important, and there are several options. The options are single, married filing jointly, married filing separately, qualified widow/widower, and head of household. The IRS defines who is single, married, head of household, or widowed. For most people, it is clear how they should file under these guidelines - but, there are some exceptions. There is some question on whether a married couple should file jointly or separately. As a general rule, if one spouse earns the vast majority of the income, then married filing jointly will provide greater tax savings. If both spouses work, married filing separately may provide greater tax savings, because it allows for more tax deductions. If a married couple is unsure, they should prepare both types of returns. This way they can determine which method provides them the greater tax savings.

## START WITH THE W-4

The IRS wants your tax money when you earn it. They want you to pay your taxes over the course of the year, as you earn your income. The W-4 is the document you submit to your employer to determine how much they should withhold from your pay for income taxes. Your employer sends this money to the IRS during the year. You can change the total amount of income withheld for taxes by adjusting the number of allowances on your W-4.

To *increase* the amount of money withheld from your pay each month, you will decrease the number of allowances on your W-4.

To *decrease* the amount of money withheld from your pay each month, you will increase the number of allowances on your W-4.

How much should you withhold from your pay each month? The IRS requires you withhold at least 90% of your taxes over the course of the year. This means if you owe $10,000 in yearly taxes, you must withhold at least $9,000 over a twelve month period. If you withhold less than 90%, you could pay an extra fee to the IRS called a *penalty*.

Because of the 90% rule, many tax-payers over-withhold each year. They do this to avoid the potential of under-withholding and paying a penalty. But, this is also a bad tax strategy. You are giving the IRS an interest-free loan over the course of the year. The money you overpay the IRS could be in your account earning interest.

Your goal should be to have the IRS withhold only the amount required over the year, and nothing more.

There are a few objections I hear to this strategy.

1. **I won't get a big refund at the end of the year, and I might even have a tax bill.** This is true. But, a tax bill at the end of the year is actually a good thing. The average American gets a $3,000 refund from the IRS when completing their taxes each year. That's a large

interest-free loan they've given to the government. If they'd kept the money during the year, they could pay down debt or earn more interest, rather than let the government use their money for free.

2. **I'm afraid I won't withhold enough, and then I'll have to pay a penalty.** This is always a possibility, but if you do your calculations right, it won't be a problem.

The IRS requires you to withhold at least 90% of your tax over the course of the year. This means you could actually under-withhold by a total of 10%, and still not pay a penalty. In fact, for 2018, the IRS has reduced this minimum withholding rule to 85%. So, for 2018 taxes, you could under-withhold 15% of your tax. You could then keep that difference until April 15, 2019.

The IRS also gives you the option of withholding an amount equal to 100% of the previous year's taxes. So, if you expect an income increase, you should only withhold an amount equal to your previous year's taxes. Keep the rest of your income until tax day. This allows you to keep a large amount of that money over the year before you pay it to the IRS.

To adjust the amount withheld from your pay, change the number of allowances on your W-4. Again, if you increase the number of allowances, you will reduce the amount withheld. If you decrease the number of allowances, you will increase the amount withheld. Use the link in Addendum (1) to estimate how many allowances to give yourself. You may pay the IRS a small tax bill at the end of the year. A good strategy is having the IRS give YOU an interest-free loan, not the other way around (TurboTax, 2018).

# 2

# Reducing Taxable Income

D uring the summer of 1996, while visiting my friend Chris in the Sunshine State, I worked at a local restaurant. It was hard work, and most of the income I received was in the form of tips from patrons. When I did my taxes that year, I was required to report the cash tips I received. I made a lot of tips!

It was very tempting at the time to not report my tips. I worked hard, why should I give my money to the government? It's easy for us to talk ourselves into being dishonest on our tax returns, but it's not a good idea. There are plenty of smart, honest strategies for reducing your taxable income, and that's the goal of this chapter. How do we get your taxable income as low as possible?

Most of your income from your employer is taxable. This is the sum included in Box 1 of the W-2 form sent to you by your employer. But, there are some fringe benefits that may be tax-free. The following are examples of common fringe benefits that may apply to you. You do not have to pay taxes for some fringe benefits. And if you don't already have some of these benefits, ask your employer if you are eligible for them. This way, you'll still get a benefit from your employer, but you won't increase your tax bill:

1. **Group term life insurance.** If your employer provides you with term life insurance coverage and the premium is less than $50,000 per year, this is tax-free.

2. **Services and discounts from your employer.** If your employer provides discounts or free services to you that he or she also provides to customers, these benefits are tax-free.

3. **Health Savings Accounts (HSA).** If your employer makes contributions to your HSA, these are tax-free.

4. **Education and retirement planning advice.** Employer-paid education is tax-free up to a certain amount. Companies are able to contribute $5,250 per year to each employee for education. This doesn't need to be job-related. It can include undergraduate college courses and graduate school. If your employer provides this benefit, it does not appear on your W-2, so it is not taxable. Retirement planning advice is also tax-free. This applies if the employer has a company-sponsored retirement plan (Kiplinger, 2018).

5. **Transportation.** Reimbursements for items such as parking and transit passes are tax-free.

6. **Other benefits.** These include adoption benefits, child care plans, tuition reductions, and working condition benefits. Refer to Addendum (2) to see all the income that can be received tax-free. Most tax software will exclude these benefits from your annual Gross Income (GI) calculation. But, it's still good to know what benefits can be received tax-free. This way, you'll know what benefits to request from your employer that you won't have to pay tax on.

One of your first goals with reducing your tax bill is reducing GI. There are certain reductions you can make to your GI to reduce your tax bill. These reductions are different than tax deductions and result in what's called your Adjusted Gross Income (AGI). Here are a few ways to make your AGI a much smaller number:

1. **Maximize your contributions to your retirement plan.** If you have a retirement plan, contribute as much as you can to it. This includes a 401(K), 403(B), or Simplified Employee Pension (SEP). This money is taken out of your pay ahead of time, so contributions are deducted from your GI (Kiplinger, 2018).

2. **Maximize your contributions to an Individual Retirement Arrangement (IRA).** If you don't have a work-sponsored retirement plan, you can contribute to an IRA. Even if you do have a work-sponsored retirement plan, you might still be able to contribute to an IRA, too. It depends on your income and the type of IRA you contribute to (Kiplinger, 2018). See Addendum (3) for the guidelines.

3. **Contribute to a SEP IRA.** Small business owners can contribute to a SEP IRA. They can contribute up to 25% of their income or $55,000, whichever is less.

4. **Contribute to an HSA.** You can use money in an HSA to pay for health-related expenses. This includes health insurance deductibles and co-pays. HSA contributions come out of your GI. You can invest this money while it's in the account, and the growth is tax-free (Kiplinger, 2018).

5. **Student Loan Interest.** If you pay student loans, and you make under $80,000 in AGI, you are eligible for deducting up to $2,500 from your tax bill. This is based on interest paid on student loans. This deduction will come out of your GI. Thus, you do not need to itemize to take advantage of this deduction.

These recommendations are designed to reduce your GI. If your resulting AGI is a much lower number, you will pay less tax. Reducing your taxable income before taking deductions is the first step in your tax saving strategy.

# 3

# Deductions and Credits

E very year for Christmas, I go back to my native home of central Pennsylvania to celebrate the holidays with family. I always look forward to spending quality time with my nieces and nephews. This includes Christmas caroling, having a drink of hot wassail, and buying gifts. Christmas morning is a much anticipated event. Every year, I can always feel the excitement among the kids, bringing me back to my own childhood memories of awaiting the special day.

Today, I view tax deductions when filing your taxes as a similar event. It's the part of tax filing that everyone looks forward to. It creates sparks of excitement as tax filers watch tax refunds increase on their returns.

Yet, the intoxicating feelings associated with a tax refund are a mirage. A refund is money you overpaid the IRS. Hence, the IRS received more money from you than what was required. Getting a refund is getting that money back, and claiming a deduction is a mechanical look at what happened in the past. Taxpayers try to see if the law will give them a tax break. It is backwards looking and reactive.

When you take a deduction on your tax return, you have a decision to make. You must decide if you will take a standard deduction or an itemized deduction. A standard deduction is a flat rate deduction. An itemized deduction is a listing of particular items that give you tax breaks. To take an itemized deduction, you must list or "itemize" what deductions you can receive. A more detailed description of both types of deductions is in the glossary.

This chapter is not a list of tax deductions or credits. You can find that information on the IRS website or in a tax reference book. This chapter proposes strategies for using tax deductions and credits to realize savings. It is a holistic way to realize long term tax savings. It is a forward-looking chapter. How can you make changes in the future to save on taxes? These strategies are proposed not so you'll get a bigger refund at the end of the year. Rather, the goal is to enable you to keep more of your money over the course of the year. You will keep more of your hard-earned money to save, invest, or spend according to your own desires, rather than put it in the hands of the tax man. Some of the strategies may not apply to your particular situation. Before adopting them, I encourage you to discuss them with a tax expert.

**1. Clumping charitable contributions.** One tax-saving strategy is to "clump" charitable contributions. Let's use an example. Kate is single and she contributes $8,000 per year to the Tragedy Assistance Program for Survivors (TAPS). The standard deduction in 2018 is $12,000 for single tax filers. Kate could continue contributing $8,000 per year. If this is her total deduction under an itemized option, then it would be smarter for her to take the standard deduction. Under the standard deduction, she would be able to deduct $12,000 from her tax bill instead of $8,000, reducing her taxable income by another $4,000.

But, if she clumps two years of charitable contributions into one year, she could save even more on her tax bill. So in year one, she saves the $8,000 she would give to TAPS, but she doesn't give it to them yet. She waits until year two, then gives both year one and year two charitable contributions in year two. In year one she takes a standard deduction of $12,000. In year two she can now take an itemized deduction of $16,000. That's an additional $4,000 deducted from her taxable income in year two.

If you use this strategy, make sure it works for the charity. If the charity needs money in the first year, you would have to compromise. But, the principle of moving some charitable money into another year is still viable.

**2. Clumping state income taxes.** Some states will allow you to pre-pay your state income tax. This is similar to clumping charitable contributions. With this strategy, you can increase your itemized tax deduction in one year. You can then elect to take the standard deduction in the following year.

Kevin is single and owes $5,000 to the State of California in income tax for 2019. He pre-paid the full amount owed for 2019 in December 2018. He also paid his 2018 state income tax of $5,000 over the course of 2018. Additionally, he made a $5,000 charitable contribution in 2018. If he itemizes his deductions, Kevin can deduct $15,000 from his 2018 federal taxable income. In 2019, he pays no state tax, and again makes charitable contributions of $5,000. He takes the standard deduction of $12,000 on his 2019 tax return. So between 2018 and 2019, he can deduct a total of $27,000 from his taxable income. If he had taken the standard deduction both years, he would have only deducted $24,000. That's a $3,000 difference.

This is a great way to save on taxes, but it doesn't work in everyone's case. Everyone's situation is different. For example, if you were required to pay the Alternative Minimum Tax (AMT), clumping state income taxes would not be beneficial. You would not realize any tax savings from that strategy. If you have questions about this, talk to a tax expert (Pender, 2017).

**3. Relocating to reduce state taxes.** In 2017, Congress placed a limit of $10,000 on deductions for state and local taxes. This includes income, sales, and property taxes. Thus, if you live in a high tax state, you may consider relocating. When many people think of relocating for tax purposes, they think they must move far. In some cases, they believe they have to move out of the state. But, one strategy may not involve moving very far. In some cases, you may even be able to stay in your current state.

A few years ago Dawn and her husband, Raymond, made a decision to move. The couple, who were residents of Old Tappan, New Jersey, loved where they lived. In fact, they were only minutes away from New York City. Their community had a high-quality public school system. But, the property taxes that came with their school system were high. Raymond's three children were now adults and no longer in school.

The couple considered moving as far as Connecticut. But, they were surprised at what they found nearby. In June 2017, they moved to the town of Saddle River, a few miles away. "We started looking and we could not believe some of the homes that we saw and the tax bracket," Dawn said. "We looked at each other in amazement. We're going to have more property, a larger home and one of them was half the taxes (Konish, 2019)."

The couple was able to bring down their tax bill—by about $10,000 every year (Konish, 2019). The lesson: If you do some research, you may be able to move a short distance and still save a lot on taxes.

**4. Giving assets away as charitable contributions.** If we give money to charity, we can get a tax deduction for it. But, if we give away an asset (such as a stock, bond, or piece of real estate), we get a tax deduction based on the *fair market value* (Kiplinger, 2018).

Let's use another example. Henry buys 100 shares of Verizon common stock. He pays $60 per share for a total investment of $6,000. In one year, the price of the stock rises to $80 per share. The fair market value of those 100 shares of stock is now $8,000. If Henry sold the stock, he would have to pay capital gains tax on the profit. The total profit would be $2,000 ($8,000 - $6,000 = $2,000). Assuming Henry owned the stock for at least one full year, the long term capital gains tax would be 15%. Thus, his tax bill would be $300 ($2,000 x 0.15 = $300). After selling the stock, Henry would have $7,700 after paying his tax ($8,000 - $300 = $7,700). He could then contribute this $7,700 to charity and get a tax deduction for that amount.

However, there's a better way to do this. If, instead of selling the stock and donating $7,700 to a charity, Henry gives the stock directly to the charity, he gets a charitable tax deduction of $8,000. He doesn't have to pay the capital gains tax because he didn't sell the stock. He also gets a larger deduction on his personal income tax bill. Assuming he is in the 32% tax bracket, he would save an extra $100 on his personal income taxes, too. By giving the stock to the charity, he would save a total of $400 in taxes, and the charity would receive an additional $300 in value.

**5. Totaling all contributions made to charity.** Many people make donations of used goods (e.g. clothing, household items, or electronics) to charity. But, they don't take a tax deduction for it. If you give something to charity, you can get a tax deduction for giving away used goods. Take note of what you give away in the future. Keep records, and you'll be able to deduct even more from your tax bill at the end of the year (McKinley, 2018). Even if you have unconventional items to give away, you can get a tax deduction based on the fair market value. This may include items such as furniture, televisions, or even motor vehicles. Several years ago, I donated a used car to the American Lung Association, and I received a $300 tax deduction for it. It may not seem like much, but small deductions can add up!

**6. Home Sale Exclusion.** When you sell your home, you may qualify for the home sale tax exclusion. This does not necessarily need to be your primary home. You must have lived in this home for at least two of the past five years before the sale. There are some other qualifying factors, too. If you are eligible, you can exclude up to $250,000 of capital gains from tax if you are single. You can exclude up to $500,000 of capital gains from tax if you are married filing jointly (Zinn, 2018). The requirement to live in the house for two years is not consecutive. Thus, you could live in the house any number of increments over the previous five years. The only requirement is that the sum of those increments equal two years. Thus, if you were using the property as a rental property, you could stay in the house when it was vacant. This is a good strategy for avoiding capital gains taxes when selling a property that is not your primary home.

**7. Medical Expenses.** You may deduct some of your unreimbursed medical and dental expenses. But, you may only deduct expenses that exceed

7.5% of your AGI. So if your AGI is $100,000, and you have $10,000 in medical or dental expenses, you would only be able to deduct $2,500. The formula is here: $100,000 x 7.5% = $7,500 and $10,000 - $7,500 = $2,500 (O'Brien, 2019). Addendum (7) lists items that are deductible medical expenses.

## DIFFERENCE BETWEEN A TAX DEDUCTION AND A TAX CREDIT

Tax deductions and tax credits are both great for your tax bill – but a tax credit is the better of the two. When you get a tax deduction, it is reducing your taxable income. Your tax bill will drop based on your highest tax bracket. When you get a tax credit, you receive a dollar amount reduction on your tax bill.

Let's use an example. Jen gets a tax deduction of $1,000. She's currently in the 22% tax bracket, so the deduction yields a savings of $220 on her tax bill. If Jen got a tax credit of $1,000 instead of a tax deduction, she'd receive a direct savings of $1,000 on her tax bill.

It's important to understand the difference between a tax deduction and a tax credit. The federal government offers several tax credits. We want to highlight the ones that can save you the most.

1. **Child Tax Credit.** You can qualify for a $2,000 tax credit for each child under age 17 you claim as a dependent. The child needs to live with you for at least half the year, and you must cover at least half of the child's living expenses. However, there may be some limits to your ability to claim the child tax credit. To get an estimate of your own situation, go to the IRS website and conduct a brief questionnaire. This will determine how much credit you can get. The child tax credit questionnaire is located here: https://www.irs.gov/help/ita/does-my-childdependent-qualify-for-the-child-tax-credit-or-the-credit-for-other-dependents.

2. **Dependent Care Credit.** If you have a dependent that does not qualify for the child tax credit because they are 17 or older, you may still be able to get credit for them of up to $500.

3. **Saver's Tax Credit.** For those married filing jointly making under $63,000 AGI, or single filers making under $31,500, the IRS will give you up to $2,000 in tax credit for some savings contributions. This depends on your income and on the amount of money you are contributing to an IRA or 401(K). Refer to Addendum (4) for the specific rules governing this tax credit and to see if you're eligible.

4. **Electric/Hybrid Vehicle Tax Credit.** You may still get up to $7,500 in tax credit for a purchase of an electric or hybrid vehicle.

There are several other tax credits you can receive, and most of them are listed in the IRS pub 17. Tax credits are more helpful than tax deductions. This is because credits are an absolute dollar reduction in your total tax bill.

# Shielding Investments

Saving for retirement can be challenging even without taxes. But I want to help you achieve this goal with tax law in mind. Many successful investors cut their tax bills whenever possible. Now this doesn't mean they buy a house just for the tax write-off. They look to cut their tax bill whenever it makes sense, including from an investing standpoint.

## MAXIMIZE THE RETIREMENT SAVINGS PLAN

Retirement plans and IRAs are your first strategies for shielding your investments. Putting as much money in your 401(K) or 403(B) is a great idea. If your employer provides you matching money, you should capture as much of the match as possible. The second priority is to maximize the account. So if you can put $19,000 in your 401(K) this year and $6,000 in a separate IRA that should be the second priority. But, you must ensure that you are getting a tax advantage by using this strategy. If your Modified Adjusted Gross Income (MAGI) is more than a certain amount, you may not be eligible to contribute to an IRA.

## NON-QUALIFIED INVESTMENTS

For investments outside your retirement accounts, you can also reduce your tax bill with these, too. These investments are called *non-qualified* investments.

## INVESTING IN TAX-DEFERRED LIFE INSURANCE

Life insurance can be important, especially if you don't have much savings and you have dependents. One type of life insurance, *permanent life*, has a cash value in addition to a death benefit. A death benefit is paid to a named beneficiary if you die. Permanent life insurance will cover your entire life. So whenever you die, your beneficiary (most likely your family) will be paid. But, permanent life also has the added benefit of having a cash value. This means that even before you die, you can access the money invested in the life insurance policy. The policy can still remain in place, even if you withdraw some of the money (Cummins, 2016).

This is important because there are some tax advantages to permanent life policies. There are many different types of permanent life policies. But we will only cover the general tax advantages. You should talk to an insurance expert or financial planner about what type of insurance is right for you. Everyone's situation is different.

Here are some of the tax advantages a permanent life insurance policy can provide:

1. **Cash value that grows tax-deferred.** A permanent life insurance policy has a cash value to it. A term life insurance policy does not have cash value. Some of the money that goes into a permanent life insurance policy is invested and earns a return. When you die your beneficiary receives the death benefit. Even if you don't die early, you can use the cash value to your advantage. When I say the cash value grows tax-deferred, this means it is not taxed while it grows. The growth is only taxed when you make withdrawals from it, and at that point, it is taxed as ordinary income. You have some control over when to make your withdrawals, and hence how much tax you pay (Cummins, 2016).

2. **Tax-free loan on your policy.** A permanent life policy would also enable you to take a loan against the cash value of the policy. This could provide a supplement to your retirement. If you took this option, you would not have to pay any income taxes. You would have to pay interest on the loan. However, these loans tend to have lower interest rates, so you would be saving on both taxes and interest (Cummins, 2016).

A permanent life insurance policy is an avenue for tax savings, but it may not necessarily be the right option for you. Talk to your financial advisor before making an investment in a policy like this.

## INVESTING IN MUNICIPAL BONDS

Municipal bonds also have tax advantages. A *bond* is a loan agreement between a lender and a borrower. *Municipal bonds*, also known as "*munis*," are bonds issued by a state or local government. In many cases, they are exempt from federal, state, and local income taxes. This means the interest you receive from one of these bonds would be tax-free. As a result, many of these bonds have a lower interest rate, or *yield*, than taxable bonds.

Holding a muni bond has tax advantages, but it usually pays a lower yield. For example, you could buy a taxable corporate bond from International Business Machines (IBM) or you could buy a muni bond from the State of Pennsylvania (PA). The IBM corporate bond pays a 6% yield. The PA muni bond pays a 4% yield. Which should you invest in?

The answer is… it depends. The IBM bond pays a higher yield, but you have to pay tax on the interest. The PA muni bond is only 4%, but you would get that interest tax-free.

Let's say you are in the 35% tax bracket. If you buy a one year $10,000 IBM bond, at the end of the year you'll get $10,600 back at a 6% yield. Now you pay 35% of that $600 in taxes. You also have to pay 10% in state and local taxes. So your tax bill is $270. You get to keep $10,330.

Now, let's say you are still in the 35% tax bracket and buy a one year $10,000 PA muni bond, but at the end of the year you get only $10,400 back. You pay zero taxes because muni bonds are not taxed. So you get to keep all $10,400. In this particular case, it would be smarter to invest in the tax-free muni bond.

But, this is not always the case. If you were in a lower tax bracket, it would be better to buy the taxable IBM bond. Muni bonds are usually advantageous for higher income tax-payers. If you have higher income, you may consider investing in muni bonds. They give tax exemption on much of their interest payments.

Each person's situation is different, so consult with your financial advisor before making the decision to invest in muni bonds. However, if used correctly, municipal bonds can provide great savings from income taxes.

## INVESTING IN EXCHANGE TRADED FUNDS (ETFS) AND MUTUAL FUNDS

Everyone, especially those new to investing, should invest in exchange traded funds (ETFs) or index funds (mutual funds) that track a broad market index. When you invest in index funds you capture the market returns and do so at the lowest cost. When you avoid selling them short term, you gain a tax advantage. In most cases you'll be paying no more than 15% in federal taxes. In some cases, you'll be paying no tax at all!

Let me give you an example. If you buy a stock or mutual fund and sell it within one year, you will pay tax on any gains. These are called *capital gains*. If you sell within one year, you'll pay tax based on your personal income tax bracket. So if you make $1,000 in profit, and you are in the 24% income tax bracket when you sell the stock, you'll pay $240 to Uncle Sam. You'll keep $760.

However, if you hang onto that stock or mutual fund for at least one year, and then sell it, you'll only pay Uncle Sam $150. You'd get to keep $850. That's almost an extra $100! Furthermore, if you are able to reduce your income tax bracket to 12% and wait a year to sell, you will pay 0%. That could mean you'd get to keep the $1,000 tax-free! Many of these stocks and mutual funds also pay dividends. *Dividends* are income paid to stock or mutual fund owners. *Qualified dividends* are taxed at the same rate as long term capital gains.

This is simpler to do than it sounds. Let's use another example. You are a single working professional, and your salary is $45,000 per year. You take the current standard deduction of $12,000. After this, you'll be in the 12% income tax bracket. Now any qualified dividends and long term capital gains you earn under $38,600 of total income will be tax-free. So, using the standard deduction, you'll reduce your taxable income to $33,000 ($45,000 - $12,000 = $33,000). Any qualified dividends and long term capital gains under $38,600 in total income will be tax-free ($38,600-$33,000 = $5,600). Thus, $5,600 of qualified dividends and long term capital gains will be tax-free.

If you are married filing jointly, and you make a salary of $70,000 per year, you can take the current standard deduction of $24,000. After this, you'll also be in the 12% tax bracket and get the same tax-free status on some of your long term capital gains, too.

## LOCKING IN LOSSES AND PAYING LOWER TAXES ON GAINS

You can use capital losses to your advantage when it comes to paying taxes. This is called tax loss harvesting. A *capital loss* is when you buy an asset and then sell it at a lower price. This is not an encouragement to lose money in the market. I want you to invest and gain money. However, this strategy can help you even if your investing goes wrong and you lose money.

For example, if you buy one investment for $4,000 and then sell it at $1,000, you would lose $3,000. This $3,000 loss would be a capital loss. If you sell the investment and take the loss within a year, you could deduct $3,000 from your ordinary taxable income. You most likely would receive a savings of $660 in taxes assuming you are in the 22% tax bracket. I say *most likely* because most readers are in the 22% tax bracket. If you are in a higher tax bracket (say the 24% or 32% bracket) your tax savings would be even greater.

If you buy an investment for $1,000 and then sell it for $4,000, the $3,000 would be a capital gain. If you sell it after more than one year, you most likely would be taxed at 15%. I say *most likely* because I'm assuming you are not in the top marginal tax bracket. If you are in the top bracket, then you would pay no more than 20% on this capital gain. Assuming you are paying 15% tax on that gain, you'd pay a total of $450 in tax. That is a net savings in taxes if you time the sale of investments. This scenario assumes you made no money on your investments (one investment increased by $3,000 and one investment decreased by $3,000). For a more detailed description of this tax saving strategy, refer to Addendum (8). Table 2 on page 20 illustrates this tax saving strategy.

## Table 2: Tax Loss Harvesting

| Asset | Purchase Price | Sale Price | Profit/Loss | Tax Bill/Credit |
|---|---|---|---|---|
| Investment #1 | $4,000 | $1,000 | -$3,000 | $660 |
| Investment #2 | $1,000 | $4,000 | $3,000 | -$450 |
| **Tax Savings** | | | | **$210** |

In the past, investors would sell a stock and then rebuy it immediately to lock in a capital loss. But, the IRS limited an investor's ability to do this. The IRS now requires a 30-day waiting period before the investor can rebuy the original stock. This is called the *wash sale rule*. If you are willing to wait the 30 days and believe the stock price will be the same, this can be a good strategy.

But, if you are uncertain you'll be able to recover the same stock, ETF, or mutual fund at a similar price in 30 days, you do have another option. You can sell one ETF or mutual fund at a loss, and immediately buy another one with a similar portfolio.

For example, you could sell an ETF that tracks the Standard and Poor's (S&P) 500 Index and buy an ETF that tracks the Dow Jones Industrial Average (DJIA). This would lock in a loss to give you a tax break, and enable you to regain the losses at a much lower tax rate in the future.

This is another great tax saving strategy. However, it may not be appropriate for you. Make sure you discuss this strategy with a tax expert or your financial advisor. They are familiar with your tax situation, and they will be able to say if this strategy is right for you.

# Tax Software and Services

When comparing tax preparation software, you have to balance cost, effectiveness, and ease of use. I'll be comparing four tax preparation software programs: TurboTax, H&R Block, FreeTaxUSA, and the IRS. Table 3 below highlights what I found as the best in each category:

## Table 3: Tax Software Comparison

| Tax Software | Cost | Effectiveness/Ease of Use |
|---|---|---|
| TurboTax | | X |
| H&R Block | | X |
| FreeTaxUSA | X | |
| IRS | X | |

I'm not promoting one service over another, but rather presenting a balanced approach to help you evaluate some of the most common software available. Use this information to decide which program is best for you.

**Least expensive.** The IRS allows you to file your taxes online with them for free assuming you have taxable income of $66,000 or less if married filing jointly, or $39,000 or less if single.

Assuming you cannot file for free with the IRS, the least expensive option is FreeTaxUSA. Federal filing is free, and state filing only costs $12.95. Some states offer free filing on their state website. Research whether your state does or not. If it does, you can do your federal taxes on FreeTaxUSA for free and then file your state taxes for free, separately through your state.

FreeTaxUSA walks you through the process very efficiently and painlessly. They go through every possible type of income, credit and deduction you could have. They are true to their word of being a free service. They don't steadily increase the price as you enter more information, and they don't try to get you to buy additional products and services you don't need.

While FreeTaxUSA is the least expensive, there were a few points in the tax-filing process where they did not adequately explain how to input information. Some of this was left up to the tax-filer to figure out. As a result, I do not give FreeTaxUSA a high mark for ease of use as I do for other tax-filing software.

If you want to file your taxes for free, one option is to file your federal taxes through FreeTaxUSA and file your state taxes separately and mail it through the post mail system. You can even use the FreeTaxUSA software to complete the state tax paperwork, and then use it as a guide to complete your state taxes manually. If you don't actually file state taxes using their service, FreeTaxUSA will not charge you.

**Ease of Use.** For this I would recommend TurboTax or H&R Block. TurboTax does an excellent job of walking you through the tax filing process. I give it a slightly higher score in ease of use than the other programs.

TurboTax and H&R Block software can be free if you meet certain income qualifications or you are a military service member. However, it makes a difference in price with H&R Block and TurboTax if you have additional forms, self-employment or contract labor income, savings account interest, an HSA, investment income, etc. FreeTaxUSA doesn't charge for entering these forms. Also TurboTax constantly recommends you upgrade to a more expensive version of their program. FreeTaxUSA does not.

## HIRING A CERTIFIED PUBLIC ACCOUNTANT (CPA)

If you already have a CPA prepare your taxes, then you can move through this section quickly. If you don't, but you are considering hiring a CPA, take your time locating a good one. Dishonest tax preparers tend to surface around tax time. Working with these people can lead to refund fraud and identity theft. It could also get you in trouble with the IRS.

Someone could pose as you—and steal your individual taxpayer identification number or Social Security number—to try to get access to your refund. And criminals are continually inventing more creative ways to get your information. Avoid this by not giving out your personal information via email, phone or text.

If someone calls threatening to arrest you, deport you or revoke your license over a tax bill, don't believe it. The IRS will never call you to demand specific payments. If you receive such a call, it is best to hang up and report the call to the IRS.

Avoid becoming a victim by doing some research on any professional with whom you work or could work. Every tax preparer should have a Preparer Tax Identification Number (PTIN) with the IRS. In addition, their registration with the agency will show whether they have appropriate qualifications, including whether they are an enrolled agent, CPA, or attorney. In addition to doing a background check on any tax preparer, be sure to carefully read your tax return before you sign it (Konish, 2019).

## ALTERNATIVE MINIMUM TAX (AMT)

The AMT is a tax triggered if certain tax benefits reduce your regular income tax below a certain level. This is computed on IRS Form 6251. So if you complete this form, and your regular income tax is below the amount calculated for you on the form, you will be required to pay the AMT.

The reason for the AMT is that many tax-payers are able to use the tax law strategically to pay no taxes. So make sure that you take a look at the AMT when you file to ensure you don't owe any additional tax according to this form.

# Tax Advantages for Military and Veterans

**M**ilitary and veterans have some additional tax advantages. The following is a list of resources for completing their tax returns:

1. **Volunteer Income Tax Assistance (VITA) services.** VITA provides assistance for military service members completing their tax returns. VITA is found on most military installations, and in some cases off-base, too (Lawhorne-Scott, 2013). VITA also provides some assistance to lower income non-military as well. For example, the Community Tax Aid (CTA) office in Washington, D.C. assists all single filers with under $30,000 gross income, and all married filing jointly with under $55,000 in gross income.

2. **TurboTax free tax service.** Intuit offers federal tax filing to certain ranks of the military free through their TurboTax software. Some discounts are offered to all ranks of the service through Intuit's partner, the United Services Automobile Association (USAA).

3. **Military One Source Financial Advising.** Military One Source offers financial counseling to active duty military, reservists, and veterans. This can be used for advice on taxes, too. However, clients should make sure they are speaking with a tax expert in any counseling session.

4. **States with income tax advantages.** Many states either have no state income tax, or they exempt military pay from state income tax if the active duty member is stationed out-of-state. Still other states exempt retired military pensions from income tax. Addendum (5) shows which states have no income tax or exempt military pensions.

5. **Combat Exclusion Zone.** If you serve in a combat zone as an enlisted service member or warrant officer for any part of a month, all military pay received for that month is excluded from gross income on your tax return. For commissioned officers, the monthly exclusion is capped at the highest enlisted pay (Lawhorne-Scott, 2013).

6. **The Thrift Savings Plan (TSP).** The TSP is a retirement savings plan available to active duty military and other federal government employees. It is similar to 401(K) plans offered by private businesses to their employees. An active duty service member can contribute up to $19,000 of their pay into a TSP account. If they elect to contribute to a traditional TSP account, that money will come out of their gross income before tax. If they elect to contribute to a Roth TSP account, the contributions will be taxed, but the growth in the account will be tax-free. For more detailed information on the TSP, refer to my book *The Blended Retirement System*.

7. **Home Sale Exclusion (for Military).** Most home-owners are familiar with the home sale exclusion. This stipulates that if you sell your home, you may exclude the first $250,000 for single filers and $500,000 for married filing jointly from your capital gains tax. The requirement is that you must have lived in the home at least two of the previous five years. This limitation does not apply to military. So military do not have to live in the home two of the previous five years in order to use the exclusion. It also does not apply to military who purchase a home, and then leave the service or retire.

# Conclusion

O ur goal with this book was two-fold: 1. Reduce your tax bill as much as possible and, 2. Have you pay your tax bill on the due date, and not a day earlier. We obviously don't cover every possible tax break in this book. However, we covered the breaks that are most likely to benefit you. We also covered tax strategies you can employ to reduce your tax bill. These are tax strategies that software or CPAs won't necessarily give you. If you want to do more extensive study on the topic of taxes, speak with a tax expert, talk to an IRS agent, or get a copy of J.K. Lasser's most updated Tax Guide. There are many resources available to assist you in saving the most on your taxes this year. If you have questions on taxes or anything in this book, please contact me at moneymissionnewsletter@gmail.com. I also encourage you to sign up for my complimentary monthly newsletter to keep you updated on personal finance topics, to include taxes. You can subscribe to my newsletter at http://patrickweinert.com. And if you want to take your financial success to the next level, join my membership program at http://patrickweinert.com/membership-registration-2/. I look forward to working with you in completing your money mission.

# Glossary

**Alimony** – Payments made to a separated or divorced spouse as required by a decree or agreement. Qualifying payments are deductible by the payer and taxable to the recipient

**Adjusted Gross Income (AGI)** – Gross Income less allowable adjustments, such as IRA deductions, alimony, and capital losses

**Alternative Minimum Tax (AMT)** – An additional tax required if a tax-payer's regular income tax falls below the tax computed on Form 6251

**Capital Gain or Loss** – Profit or loss resulting from the sale of an asset

**Capital Loss Carryover** – A capital loss that is not deductible because it exceeds the annual $3,000 capital loss ceiling. A carryover loss may be deducted from capital gains of later years plus up to $3,000 of ordinary income.

**Certified Public Accountant (CPA)** – Qualified accountants licensed to provide accounting services to the public

**Deductions** – Items directly reducing income. Personal deductions such as mortgage interest, state taxes, and charitable contributions are allowed only if deductions are itemized. Deductions such as alimony, capital losses, student loan interest, and IRA contributions are deducted from Gross Income even if itemized deductions are not claimed.

**Gross Income (GI)** – Total income received from all sources before exclusions and deductions

**Individual Retirement Arrangement (IRA)** – A retirement account which is given special tax-favored treatment and to which a designated amount of savings may be contributed

**Internal Revenue Service (IRS)** – The United States federal government's tax collection agency

**Itemized Deductions** – Items such as interest, state income taxes, and charitable contributions claimed on Schedule A of Form 1040. Itemized deductions are subtracted from AGI to determine taxable income.

**Modified Adjusted Gross Income (MAGI)** – AGI that has been increased by certain items

**Ordinary Income** – Income other than long-term capital gains or qualified dividends

**Penalty** – a fine paid to the IRS for paying taxes late

**Preparer Tax Identification Number (PTIN)** – A preparer tax identification number required for tax professionals to prepare tax returns for compensation

**Qualified Dividends** – Dividends that are taxed at the long-term capital gains rate

**Standard Deduction** – A fixed deduction allowed to taxpayers who do not itemize deductions

**Tax Deferral** – Shifting an income tax to a later year

**Tax Loss Harvesting** – Selling securities at a loss to offset a capital gains tax

**Taxable Income** – Remaining income after claiming all deductions from AGI

**Yield** – Interest or dividend income from an investment

# Addenda

**Addendum (1): Formula for Allowances.** The IRS provides an allowance calculator in order to help you determine the number of allowances you should have on your W-4. Access the allowance calculator at this link: https://www.irs.gov/individuals/irs-withholding-calculator.

**Addendum (2): Tax-free Fringe Benefits.** The following is a list of employer-provided benefits that an employee may receive tax-free. For specific restrictions on each type of tax-free benefit, visit the IRS website at www.irs.gov.

1. Adoption benefits
2. Athletic facilities
3. Child or dependent care plans
4. Discounts on company products or services
5. Education plans
6. Employee achievement awards
7. Group-term life insurance
8. Health and accident plans including HSAs
9. Interest-free or low-interest loans
10. Moving expense reimbursements for U.S. military
11. Retirement planning advice
12. Transportation benefits
13. Tuition reductions
14. Working condition benefits (Lasser, 2019)

**Addendum (3): Rules governing IRA contributions.** In order to receive a tax deduction for contributions to a traditional IRA, you must meet certain Modified Adjusted Gross Income (MAGI) requirements. Refer to Publication 590A page 13 for details. You can find this publication at www.irs.gov. In order to contribute to a Roth IRA, you must have taxable compensation for personal services and your MAGI does not exceed the upper end of the phase-out range for your filing status. For further guidance, reference Publication 590A or contact the IRS at (800) 829-1040.

**Addendum (4): Rules governing the saver's tax credit.** You are only eligible for the saver's tax credit if your adjusted gross income (AGI) does not exceed $63,000 if married filing jointly, $47,250 if head of household, and $31,500 if single, married filing separately, or a qualified widow/widower.

**Addendum (5): States with Income Tax Advantages for Military.** The following states either have no income tax, or they do not tax military pensions. The first nine states in the list have no income tax.

1. Alaska
2. Florida
3. Nevada
4. New Hampshire
5. South Dakota
6. Tennessee
7. Texas
8. Washington
9. Wyoming
10. Alabama
11. Arkansas
12. Connecticut
13. Hawaii
14. Illinois
15. Iowa

16. Kansas
17. Louisiana
18. Maine
19. Massachusetts
20. Michigan
21. Minnesota
22. Mississippi
23. Missouri
24. New Jersey
25. New York
26. Ohio
27. Pennsylvania
28. West Virginia
29. Wisconsin

## Addendum (6): Changes to Personal Income Taxes in 2018.

Several changes were made to the federal tax code with the passage of the Tax Cuts and Jobs Act of 2017. Below, I've listed the main changes to the tax law. There are a few items I've excluded for simplicity (such as changes to the corporate tax law), but the following are the changes that likely affect you the most.

1. *Income Tax Brackets.* 2018 tax brackets are listed in Table 1 on page 2.

2. *Standard Deduction*
Old Rule: Taxpayers who do not itemize can claim the current standard deduction of $6,350 for single individuals, $9,350 for heads of household or $12,700 for married couples filing jointly.

New Rule: Standard deductions for all nearly double under the new rules. Individuals see standard deductions rise to $12,000; for heads of household, it rises to $18,000; and for married couples filing jointly the standard deduction increases to $24,000.

### 3. *State and Local Tax Deduction*
<u>Old Rule</u>: Taxpayers may include state and local property, income, and sales taxes as itemized deductions.

<u>New Rule</u>: Taxpayers are limited to claiming an itemized deduction of $10,000 in combined state and local income, sales and property taxes, starting in 2018 through 2025.

### 4. *Medical Expense Tax Deduction*
<u>Old Rule</u>: Taxpayers were previously allowed to deduct out-of-pocket medical expenses that exceed 10 percent of their adjusted gross income or 7.5 percent if they or their spouse were 65 or older.

<u>New Rule</u>: The threshold for all taxpayers to claim an itemized deduction for medical expenses is lowered to 7.5 percent of a filer's adjusted gross income. The change applies to taxable years from Dec. 31, 2016 to Jan. 1, 2019.

### 5. *Affordable Care Act (ACA) Individual Mandate*
<u>Old Rule</u>: Consumers who did not qualify for an exemption and chose not to purchase health insurance faced a range of tax penalties, depending on income.

<u>New Rule</u>: The individual mandate is repealed. This is starting Jan. 1, 2019. After that date, consumers who do not purchase health insurance will no longer face penalties.

### 6. *529 College Savings Plan*
<u>Old Rule</u>: 529 plan savings could only be used on qualified higher education expenses.

<u>New Rule</u>: You can now use 529 savings for private K-12 schooling. Tax benefits are now extended to eligible education expenses for an elementary or secondary public, private, or religious school. The new rules allow you to withdraw up to $10,000 a year per student (child) for education costs.

### 7. Personal Exemption

Old Rule: Taxpayers can reduce their adjusted gross income (AGI) by claiming personal exemptions—generally for the taxpayer, their spouse and their dependents.

New Rule: The deduction is phased out for taxpayers earning more than certain AGI thresholds. The phase out begins at an AGI over $313,800 for married couples filing jointly, $287,650 for heads of household, $156,900 for married couples filing separately and $261,500 for all other taxpayers. Personal exemptions have been suspended through 2025.

### 8. Alimony

Old Rule: The individual paying alimony or maintenance payments can deduct payments from their income. The person receiving the payments includes them as income.

New Rule: The person making alimony or maintenance payments does not get to deduct them, and the recipient does not claim the payments as income. This goes into effect for any divorce or separation agreement signed or modified on or after Jan. 1, 2019.

### 9. Child Tax Credit

Old Rule: The current child tax credit is $1,000 per child under the age of 17. The credit is reduced by $50 for each $1,000 a taxpayer earns over certain thresholds. The phase-out thresholds start at a modified AGI over $75,000 for single individuals and heads of household, $110,000 for married couples filing jointly and $55,000 for married couples filing separately.

New Rule: The child tax credit doubles to $2,000 per qualifying child. Up to $1,400 of the child tax credit can be received as refundable credit (meaning it can go toward a tax refund). The new rule also includes a $500 nonrefundable credit per dependent other than a qualifying child. The credit begins to phase out at an AGI over $200,000—for married couples, the phase-out starts at an AGI over $400,000. This rule is in effect through 2025.

10. *Mortgages*

<u>Old Rule</u>: Currently homeowners are allowed to deduct interest paid on mortgages valued up to $1 million on a taxpayer's principal residence and one other qualified residence. They can also deduct interest paid on a home equity loan or home equity line of credit no greater than $100,000. These are itemized deductions.

<u>New Rule</u>: New homeowners can include mortgage interest paid on up to $750,000 of principal value on a new home in their itemized deductions. The old, $1 million caps continues to apply to current homeowners (those who took out their mortgages on or before Dec. 15, 2017), as well as refinancing on mortgages taken out on or before Dec. 15, 2017, as long as new mortgage amount does not exceed the amount of debt being refinanced. Homeowners CAN deduct interest paid on a home equity line of credit or home equity loan, so long as the loan was used to buy, build or substantially improve your home. These changes are set to expire after 2025.

11. *Estate Tax*

<u>Old Rule</u>: Estates up to $5.49 million in value were exempt from the tax. The top tax rate was 40 percent.

<u>New Rule</u>: Doubles the exemption for the estate tax. Now, estates up to $11.2 million are exempt from the tax.

No change to the following deductions: teacher deduction, electric cars, adoption assistance, or student loan interest deduction.

**Addendum (7): List of deductible medical and dental expenses.** For a more detailed list of deductible expenses, refer to the IRS website at www.irs.gov.

1. Professional services
2. Dental services
3. Equipment and supplies

4. Medical treatments
5. Medicines and drugs
6. Laboratory examinations and tests
7. Premiums for medical care policies
8. Other miscellaneous costs (Lasser, 2019)

## Addendum (8): Description of tax loss harvesting strategy.

Henry buys 100 share of Verizon common stock for $60 per share. His total investment is $6,000. He sells the shares 6 months later for $10 per share, and recovers $1,000. However, he lost $5,000 because he paid $6,000 for the stock. This $5,000 loss is known as a capital loss.

Since Henry sold the stock within a year of buying it, it qualifies as a short term capital loss. Therefore, Henry can deduct the total amount of the loss from his GI this year. This changes his AGI. It is not a tax deduction.

The reason this is significant is because you can use it to strategically save on taxes.

Henry makes an AGI of $70,000 per year and he takes the standard deduction. Therefore he is taxed at 22% on his income between $38,600 and $58,000.

If he sells the Verizon stock and takes a $5,000 loss within the year, he reduces his AGI by $5,000 down to $65,000. This reduces his tax bill of 22% on $5,000. So he realizes an immediate tax savings of $1,100.

There are two rules to keep in mind with this tax loss harvesting strategy:

First, Henry can only claim a maximum of $3,000 of his losses against ordinary income this year. If he has at least $2,000 in capital gains this year, he can take the full $5,000 reduction in his taxable income, but only $3,000 applies to his ordinary income. If he has no capital gains this year, he will only take a $3,000 reduction to his taxable income this year. He will be able to deduct the remaining $2,000 in ordinary income next year. This is called a capital loss carryover.

Second, Henry is required by law to wait 30 days before he can repurchase the same stock he sold. He waits 30 days (still within the calendar year) and then re-buys the same 100 shares of stock for $1,000.

He now waits over one year, and sells the stock back at $60 per share for a total of $6,000. He has recovered his lost $5,000. But since he waited over a year to sell it, it is taxed at 15% as a long term capital gain. So he only pays $750 in tax. He saved $1,100 in year one, and paid $750 in year two. So he saved a total of $350 in taxes based on one investment in which he broke even.

# References

Cummins, B. (2016, February 22). "Using Tax Advantages of Life Insurance in Your Financial Plan." Retrieved from https://www.nerdwallet.com/blog/insurance/life-insurance-in-your-financial-planning/

Galles, G. (1993, February 8). "How Speed Limits Can Cost Lives." *Chicago-Tribune.* Retrieved from https://www.chicagotribune.com/news/ct-xpm-1993-02-08-9303176834-story.html

Konish, L. (2019, February 12). "Don't lose your refund—or your shirt—to these common tax scams." Retrieved from https://www.cnbc.com/2019/02/12/dont-lose-your-refund--to-these-common-tax-scams.html

Konish, L. (2019, February 16). "One surprising way to beat the SALT deduction cap: Move to a nearby town." Retrieved from https://www.cnbc.com/2019/02/15/beat-the-salt-cap-deduction-by-moving-to-a-nearby-town.html

Lasser, J. (2019). *Your Income Tax 2019.* Hoboken, N.J., John Wiley & Sons, Inc.

Lawhorne-Scott, C. and Philpot, D. (2013). *Military Finances.* Lanham, Maryland, Rowman & Littlefield Publishers, Inc.

McKinley, J. (2018). "17 Tax Deductions You Can't Afford to Miss." *Reader's Digest.* Retrieved from https://www.rd.com/advice/tax-deductions-you-cant-miss/

No Author. (2018, August 10) "14 Ways for Everyone to Save on Taxes Under the New Tax Law." Retrieved from https://www.kiplinger.com/slideshow/taxes/T054-S011-ways-for-everyone-to-save-on-taxes-under-the-new-t/index.html

No Author. (2018). "Fatten Your Paycheck and Still get a Tax Refund."

Retrieved from https://turbotax.intuit.com/tax-tips/tax-refund/fatten-your-paycheck-and-still-get-a-tax-refund/L5HaySdDP

O'Brien, S. (2019, 14 February). "High health-care costs could get you a tax break on your 2018 return." Retrieved from https://www.cnbc.com/2019/02/14/high-health-care-costs-could-get-you-a-tax-break-on-your-2018-return.html

Pender, K. (2017, December 28). "Should you prepay your state income and property taxes?" Retrieved from https://www.sfchronicle.com/business/networth/article/Should-you-prepay-your-state-income-and-property-12448762.php

Zinn, D. (2018, December 13). "How to avoid paying capital gains tax when selling your home." Retrieved from https://www.bankrate.com/finance/taxes/capital-gains-and-your-home-sale-1.aspx

# About the Author

Patrick Weinert is founder and CEO of The Money Mission L.L.C., where he educates and helps customers manage their personal finances. He is author of several additional books, including *The Money Mission, The Blended Retirement System*, and *Financial Abundance*. Weinert served twenty years as a United States Marine Corps officer and mentored hundreds of service members in personal finance. He also served as advisor to the Chief Financial Officer of the Marine Corps. He received a bachelor's degree in economics and political science from Christendom College and a master's degree in management with a business focus from the University of Maryland. Weinert currently lives in Washington, D.C., where he enjoys running, biking, reading, writing, and supporting charitable causes.